WILD
DISGUISES

BY VIRGINIA LOH-HAGAN

45th Parallel Press

Published in the United States of America by Cherry Lake Publishing Group
Ann Arbor, Michigan
www.cherrylakepublishing.com

Reading Adviser: Beth Walker Gambro, MS Ed., Reading Consultant, Yorkville, IL
Book Designer: Melinda Millward

Library of Congress Cataloging-in-Publication Data

Names: Loh-Hagan, Virginia, author.
Title: Wild disguises / written by Virginia Loh-Hagan.
Description: Ann Arbor, Michigan : Cherry Lake Publishing, [2023] | Series: Wild Wicked Wonderful Express. | Includes index.
   | Audience: Grades 2-3 | Summary: "Which animals have the wildest disguises? This book explores the wild, wicked, and
   wonderful world of animal disguises. Series is developed to aid struggling and reluctant young readers with engaging high-
   interest content, considerate text, and clear visuals. Includes table of contents, glossary with simplified pronunciations, index,
   sidebars, and author biographies"—Provided by publisher.
Identifiers: LCCN 2022043127 | ISBN 9781668920718 (paperback) | ISBN 9781668919699 (hardcover) |
   ISBN 9781668922040 (ebook) | ISBN 9781668923375 (pdf)
Subjects: LCSH: Camouflage (Biology)—Juvenile literature. | Mimicry (Biology)—Juvenile literature. | Animal defenses—Juvenile
   literature. | Animals—Adaptation—Juvenile literature.
Classification: LCC QL767 .L678 2023 | DDC 591.47/2—dc23/eng/20221018
LC record available at httA://lccn.loc.gov/2022043127

Cherry Lake Publishing Group would like to acknowledge the work of the Partnership for 21st Century Learning,
a Network of Battelle for Kids. Please visit http://www.battelleforkids.org/networks/p21 for more information.

Printed in the United States of America

About the Author
Dr. Virginia Loh-Hagan is an author, university professor, former classroom teacher, and curriculum designer.
She's not good at disguises. Her loud laugh gives her away. She lives in San Diego with her very tall
husband and very naughty dogs.

Table of Contents

Introduction

Animals change colors. They change shapes. They blend in. They act like something else. They **disguise** themselves. To disguise means to change your looks or sound. Disguises help animals hide.

Animals mislead **prey**. Prey are animals that are hunted for food. Animals mislead **predators**. Predators are hunters. Animals are experts at **deception**. Deception means tricking others.

Animals also disguise themselves to hunt for food. Animals want to **survive**. Survive means to stay alive.

Some animals have extreme disguises. Their disguises are bigger. Their disguises are better. They have the most exciting disguises in the animal world!

Animals disguise themselves in different ways.

Lyrebirds

Lyrebirds live in rainforests. They live in Australia. They can disguise their voices.

Lyrebirds sing all year. They sing the most from June to August. They sing for 4 hours each day. Male lyrebirds can copy more than 20 different birdcalls. They also copy non-bird sounds. Examples include a camera, car alarm, and chainsaw.

Male lyrebirds have a beautiful tail.
It is used to attract mates.

The "lyre" in lyrebird comes from the ancient Greek instrument. A lyre is like a U-shaped harp.

Lyrebirds also can sound like humans. Females also make sounds. But they're not as skilled as males. Young birds take about a year to learn sounds.

Males sing to attract mates. The best singer gets the most females. Their songs combine their own songs and other noises.

When Animals Attack!

Alligator snapping turtles live in the United States. They're the largest freshwater turtles. They can grow up to 300 pounds (136 kilograms). They have powerful jaws and sharp claws. They have a special hunting move. They lie still in the water. They disguise themselves as rocks. They open their jaws. Their tongues look like worms. They trick small fish, frogs, and other turtles. When prey enter their mouths, they snap their jaws shut. They instantly kill their prey.

Arctic Foxes

Arctic foxes live in the Arctic. They have white fur. This is how they stay alive. They **camouflage**. Camouflage means to blend in with the surroundings. Arctic foxes blend in with snow. They hide. They hunt. They avoid predators.

They get close to polar bears. They eat the polar bears' leftovers. But they don't go too close. They don't want the polar bears to eat them!

Arctic foxes shed their fur in summer. They lose their white coats. The summer coats have different colors.

Arctic foxes turn white in the winter.

Sea Snakes

Sea snakes mostly live in the Pacific Islands. Most have black and white stripes. Sea snakes weave through the water. They trick the eyes.

Sea snake heads and tails are black. Predators can't tell what direction it's going. Predators can't tell where the snake's head is. They think the snake is attacking from behind. This gives the snake time. It can swim away. Or it can fight.

Sea snakes are venomous. The venom can kill a person in 15 minutes to 24 hours.

There are very few animals in the sea brave enough to take on a sea snake.

Spider Crabs

Spider crabs live on the ocean floor. They're known as "camouflage crabs." They're bumpy. They blend into the rocky floor.

They have claws called **pincers**. Their pincers are long and narrow. They wave them over their heads. This warns off predators.

Spider crabs range in size. Adult males are larger than females.

Spider crabs can have a leg span of up to 12 feet (3.8 meters).

Spider crabs are slower and weaker than other crabs. They create disguises. They hide. They use their pincers. They trim plant pieces. They chew them. They stick the chewed ends to their bodies. They have tiny hairs on their legs and back. The hairs look like hooks. Spider crabs stick the plants to their hairs. They blend in. They look like plants.

Humans
Do What?!?

Tom Leppard was known as "Leopard Man." His real name was Tom Wooldridge. Wooldridge lived in Scotland. He tattooed his skin. He made himself look like a leopard. He had a world record. He was the world's most tattooed male senior citizen. Tom even lived like a leopard. He lived in a small hut with a dirt floor. He was far away from town. He didn't have electricity. He cooked on a small gas stove.

Walking Sticks

Walking sticks are bugs. Their tails look like twigs. Their legs look like leaves or sticks.

They're **nocturnal**. This means they're active at night. During the day, they're still. They look like branches. They sit on bark. They don't move. They copy their surroundings. They're green or brown. This protects them. They don't want to be eaten by birds.

Giant walking sticks can be more than 21 inches (53 centimeters). They're one of the world's longest insects.

Walking sticks used to be believed to bring good fortune and good luck! People wanted to keep them in their homes.

Walking sticks do many things to escape predators. They pretend to be dead. They sometimes shed their legs. Some release bad-smelling liquid.

Baby walking sticks disguise themselves as ants. They copy how ants move. They copy how ants look. Ants are known for attacking other bugs.

Did You Know...?

- The banded snake eel is a fish disguised as a snake. It looks and moves like a snake. Predators don't like to mess with snakes.

- Walking sticks lose limbs. They can grow new ones. Some walking sticks squirt liquid at predators. They blind predators.

- Some octopuses can use tools. They find coconut shells. They play with them. They use the shells as shelter.

Octopuses

Octopuses live at the bottom of the ocean. They don't have bones. They can squeeze through tight places.

They use camouflage. They hide. They can change shape, color, and skin **texture**. Texture is the feel of something. This makes their disguise more real. They can change in less than a second.

Mimic octopuses pretend to be other animals. Mimic means to copy. The octopuses copy shapes and movements. They copy speed.

Octopuses have many disguises. See how this one tries to blend in?

Consider This!

Take a Position! Animal disguises help prey. They help predators. Do you think disguises benefit prey or predators more? Why or why not?

Think About It! How do humans use disguises? In what ways are we similar to the animals featured in this book?

Learn More
- **Article:** National Geographic Kids - "Stick Insect." November 4, 2015: https://kids.nationalgeographic.com/animals/invertebrates/facts/stick-insect.
- **Book:** Weber, Belinda. 2017. Animal Disguises. London ; New York: Kingfisher.

Glossary

camouflage (KA-muh-flaj) to blend into the surroundings

deception (dih-SEP-shuhn) the act of misleading

disguise (dih-SKYZ) something that changes appearance

mimic (MIH-mihk) copy

nocturnal (nahk-TUR-nuhl) active at night

pincers (PIHN-surz) claws

predators (PREH-duh-turz) animals that hunt other animals for food

prey (PRAY) animals hunted for food

survive (sur-VYV) stay alive

texture (TEKS-chur) the feel of something

Index